TABLE OF CONTENTS

IS MAKING YOUR HOME MORE ENERGY EFFICIENT THE RIGHT STEP FOR YOU?

Why older manufactured homes are good candidates for energy efficiency retrofits:

- *All homes experience wear and tear.* Whether your home is five or 50 years old, chances are good that it can benefit from cost-effective measures to improve its energy efficiency. Wind, vibrations, sunlight and seasonal temperature changes can loosen up a tight home, increasing air leakage; windows may no longer close tightly, and ductwork can spring leaks, wasting huge amounts of heating or cooling energy. Furnaces, air conditioners, and water heaters that have been running for years gradually lose efficiency, especially if regular cleaning and maintenance hasn't been done. All these things add up!

- *Technologies change.* While your manufactured home may have been built to the energy standards of the time, dramatic progress has been made over the past few decades with high-efficiency mechanical equipment, insulation, windows, and so forth. Our understanding of how to retrofit manufactured homes for energy savings has also improved through years of experience—as has our knowledge of how to prevent moisture problems.

- *Energy costs are going up.* Whether you use electricity, natural gas, propane, or oil, many experts believe that prices will continue to rise. Improving your home now guards against future increases, and rolls back the costs you're paying today.

Five good reasons why an energy retrofit makes sense:

- Lower energy and homeownership costs

- Protection against future increases in energy costs

- Improved comfort—Fewer drafts, more comfortable temperatures, less temperature fluctuation floor-to-ceiling and from room to room, less chance of moisture problems

- Increased resale value—A home with lower operating costs is worth more

- Environmental stewardship—Saving energy reduces the burning of fossil fuels that contributes to global warming, acid rain, smog and other kinds of pollution

How to tell if you can benefit from improving your home's energy performance:

Your home is a good candidate for upgrade if:

- You have significantly higher utility bills than neighbors with similar homes and lifestyles.

- Your home was built before 1994 (and especially before 1976) and hasn't been significantly improved or upgraded.

- Your heating, cooling, or water heating equipment breaks down a lot.

- You feel drafts inside on windy days.

- The air near the floor is significantly cooler than the air near the ceiling.

- You have to wait a long time for hot water, and water cools off quickly between uses.

- You have to set the thermostat below 70° to stay cool in the summer.

- You have trouble keeping your home warm in winter or cool in summer.

- There are large fluctuations in your utility bills from month to month, and especially from the same month of the previous year.

- There is condensation on the inside surface of your windows in the winter.

USING THIS GUIDE

The energy efficiency retrofit ideas described in this guide have been selected because they provide excellent energy savings. In general, more expensive techniques result in greater savings, but the inexpensive techniques described here can also lower your energy bills substantially. This guide will help you choose the most cost-effective ways to reduce energy use that fit your budget and your home's characteristics and location. There are many ways to save energy and reduce costs. The techniques covered here provide exceptional value for owners of manufactured homes; most techniques will pay for themselves relatively quickly through energy savings.

The retrofit techniques are divided into ten categories shown in Table 2. Each category contains a number of related techniques. In general, the top item(s) in each category are easier to complete and cost less. The techniques in the latter categories typically require greater skill and cost more, but they also provide greater energy savings.

Table 2 also indicates the approximate cost and skill level of each technique and the climate in which that technique is most appropriate. Although energy bills can vary from home to home, in general, you're in a colder climate if your energy bills are highest in winter, and you're in a hotter climate if your power bills are higher in summer. An explanation of the symbols used in the table and throughout the guide is provided below.

Table 1

Table 1. Key to symbols describing each energy-savings technique

Feature	Symbol	Definition
Energy Savings	☆	This technique provides exceptional energy savings relative to its cost.
Approximate Cost[1]	FREE	No cost
	$	Cost less than $100
	$$	Cost between $100 and $500
	$$$	Cost over $500
Skill[2]	Low	No skill required; for example, changing a light bulb or a filter.
	Medium	Ability to use basic tools and follow directions; for example, installing water heater insulation wrap.
	High	Must be very handy; for example, fabricating and installing a simple storm window.
	PRO	Requiring professional skills and equipment; for example, installing insulation in the walls.

⚠ Especially important information or cautions about things to avoid or risks of certain techniques.

 Tip for additional energy savings or other benefits.

---

[1] Costs are rough approximations and will vary depending on the size and condition of your home as well as the specific products and techniques chosen to implement the energy-saving retrofit measure. For do-it-yourself measures this is the cost of materials only. If the technique is listed as PRO (requiring professional assistance) then it is the fee charged by the contractor.

[2] This is a rough estimate of the skill level required to install a given measure.

Table 2

Category • Technique	Home Climate	Approximate Cost	Skill	Page Number
1. Improve heating system performance [1]				**6**
• Clean or replace the furnace filter ☆	All	FREE or $	Low	6
• Have a pro maintain and tune up the furnace ☆	All	$	Pro	7
• Replace the furnace	All	$$$	Pro	7
2. Improve cooling system performance [2]				**9**
• Clean or replace the air filter ☆	All	FREE or $	Low	9
• Clean the condensing cooling coils	All	FREE	Medium	10
• Have a pro perform seasonal maintenance ☆	All	$	Pro	10
• Replace the air conditioning system	All	$$$	Pro	10
• Other techniques to reduce air conditioner energy cost	All	FREE or $	Low	11
3. Eliminate leaks in ducts				**12**
• Seal supply duct connections to boots, and registers ☆	All	$	Medium	13
• Seal duct ends ☆	All	$	Medium	13
• Make sure all registers are fully open ☆	All	FREE	Low	14
• Seal and insulate crossover duct and connections ☆	All	$	High	14
• Inspect and repair ducts from under the home ☆	All	$	High	15
• Seal beneath the furnace	All	$	High-Pro	15
4. Improve lighting efficiency				**17**
• Replace incandescent light bulbs with CFLs ☆	All	$	Low	17
• Install energy-saving controls on exterior lights	All	$	Medium	18
• Clean fixtures	All	FREE	Low	18
• Use low-wattage light bulbs	All	$	Low	18
5. Improve refrigerator performance				**19**
• Operate your existing refrigerator properly	All	FREE or $	Low	19
• Buy a new refrigerator	All	$$-$$$	Low	20
6. Improve water heater performance				**21**
• Insulate the tank ☆	All	$	Medium	21
• Insulate water pipes leading from the tank ☆	All	$	Low	22
• Lower the water heater thermostat ☆	All	FREE	Low	22
• Clean the tank	All	FREE	Medium	22
• Install low-flow showerheads and faucet aerators	All	$	Low	23
• Replace your water heater	All	$$	Pro	23
7. Reduce solar heat				**24**
• Install sun screens	All	$$	High	24
• Install exterior awnings	All	$$-$$$	Medium	24
• Apply reflective window film	All	$$	High	25
• Use interior shades to block sunlight	All	$$	Medium	26
• Install a reflective roof coating	All	$$$	Pro	26
8. Improve window performance				**27**
• Install interior storm windows ☆	Colder	$$-$$$	Medium-High	28
• Install plastic disposable window insulating kits	Colder	$	Low	28
9. Eliminate leaks in the walls, floor and ceiling				**29**
• Patch/replace torn or missing bottom board ☆	All	$	Medium	29
• Seal gaps and cracks in the walls, floor and ceiling	All	$	Medium	30
• Cover window air conditioners	All	FREE or $	Low	31
• Seal leaky windows	All	$	Low	31
• Fix poorly fitting exterior doors	All	$	Medium	31
10. Insulate walls, floor and ceiling				**32**
• Add insulation to the floor	All	$$$	Pro	33
• Add insulation to the roof	All	$$$	Pro	33
• Add insulation to sidewalls	Colder	$$$	Pro	34

[1] This recommendation applies to all but the hottest climates.

[2] This recommendation applies to all but the coldest climates.

The next section describes each technique in detail, including:

Table 3. Getting help—a list of programs that offer financial and other assistance

- How to tell if the technique makes sense for you by describing where the technique has the most benefit.

- The level of skill required—whether the project is suitable for a homeowner to perform (and if so, the level of skill required), or if it requires professional assistance.

- Enough detail for you to carry out a simple do-it-yourself (DIY) technique—or for more complex projects, a basic description of what a professional contractor will do and where to get more information.

- Approximate costs of doing the project.

A list of common-sense, low-cost or no-cost lifestyle tips that you can implement today to lower your energy bills appears on page 35. A list of resources for additional information is provided on page 37.

Table 3

Program	How to Contact	What They Can Do
Weatherization Assistance Program	www.eere.energy.gov/weatherization Yellow Pages under "weatherization"	Free home weatherization for qualified applicants; often have long waiting lists.
State energy offices	www.eere.energy.gov/states	Find energy efficiency resources by state.
Home Performance with ENERGY STAR®	www.energystar.gov	Refer you to a qualified contractor.
Utilities	Contact your power company	Some utilities offer rebates or other incentives for energy efficiency upgrades.
Municipal programs	Yellow Pages under city, country, or town	Available in some areas.

Each chapter includes a description of an energy-saving tip, the goal of the tip—or what you will achieve-indicators that will help you determine whether the tip makes sense for your home, and various techniques to achieve the goal.

Selecting a professional contractor

When selecting a professional contractor, choose one who has experience with the specialized techniques and construction characteristics of manufactured homes. Your state's Weatherization Assistance Program (see Table 3) may be able to direct you to a list of potential contractors. You can also locate contractors through your electric utility, manufactured home retailer, and the yellow pages or by talking to neighbors. Always choose licensed contractors and check their references. Select a contractor with a track record of satisfied customers and plenty of experience with your type of project.

Questions to ask a contractor

Ask for a written estimate of the work based on a set of plans and/or written specifications. If you are comparing estimates, be sure they are based on the same specifications and scope of work. Beware of an exceptionally low price. Find out whether the contractor uses a detailed, written contract. The contract should spell out the work that will and will not be performed and provide a fair payment schedule. Ask contractors if they offer a warranty, and if so, what kind and for how long. Professional contractors should carry insurance that protects you from claims arising from property damage or jobsite injuries. Ask for a copy of the contractor's insurance certificate.

Doublecheck the contractor's qualifications

Check with your local or state office of consumer protection and the local Better Business Bureau. Ask if they have had any complaints about the contractor and if so, whether they were resolved satisfactorily. Check with your state's licensing agency and the state and local building inspectors to see if they have received any complaints about the contractor and to verify that the contractor has the appropriate licenses and registrations.

1 IMPROVE HEATING SYSTEM PERFORMANCE

Description

Most manufactured home heating systems have two main parts: a furnace that heats air, and ducts that channel the heated air throughout the home. This section discusses the furnace.

The furnace—often located inside a closet—generates heat by burning natural gas, propane, or oil, or by using electricity. Heated air from the furnace is then blown through ducts (which may be under the floor or in the attic), and finally through registers or grates into various rooms.

Goal

A heating system that operates efficiently reduces energy use while providing the necessary comfort. High efficiency is important, particularly in colder climates. There are several components in a manufactured home heating system that need to be properly maintained. Following the tips in this guide will keep your heating system running smoothly and efficiently, and increase its lifespan.

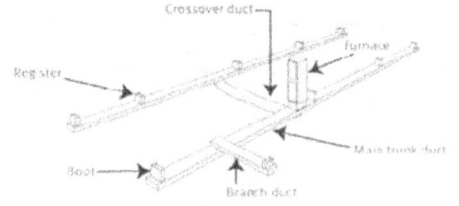

Typical floor duct system

Indicators

If you answer YES to any of these questions, heating system maintenance is especially important for your home:

- Are you in a colder climate?
- Do you find it difficult to keep your home warm in the winter?
- Does your heating system experience frequent breakdowns?
- Is one part of the house much colder than others?
- Do you use a space heater to supplement your heating system?
- For combustion furnaces only, can you see soot near the roof jack (chimney) cap?

  This may indicate improper flame adjustment.

Techniques

There are some simple things you can do yourself to make sure your heating system operates smoothly; other actions require the help of a professional. For older heating systems, replacement may be the best option.

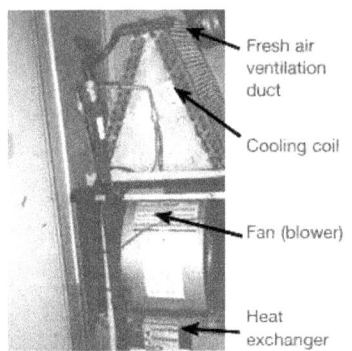

Fresh air ventilation duct

Cooling coil

Fan (blower)

Heat exchanger

Inside a typical electric furnace closet

Clean or replace the furnace filter ☆
(FREE or $, low skill)

Filters help keep the furnace's heat exchanger and blower clean by removing dust from your home's air. Furnace filters are generally made of fiberglass or plastic fibers, or porous foam that allows air to pass through. Return air from the house is filtered as it is pulled through the filter.

⚠ *Installing a filter.*
When installing the new filter, make sure the air-flow arrow on the filter points the right way.

⚠ *Clean the filter.*
It is especially important to clean pleated filters at least monthly. These filters are more efficient at removing dust, so they get dirty more quickly than conventional filters, which can lead to less efficient operation and shorter furnace life.

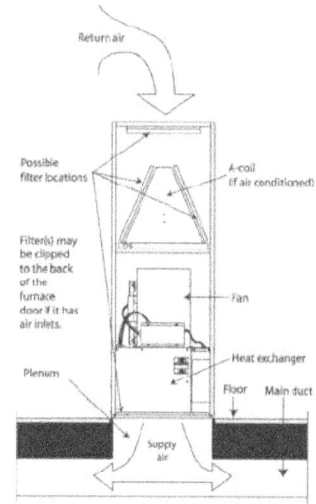

Possible furnace filter locations

Dirty filters reduce the efficiency of your furnace by restricting airflow. Some filters are designed to be vacuumed or washed, but most are disposable and need to be replaced when they become clogged. Replacement is an easy task that most homeowners can do themselves. Some high efficiency filters might also restrict airflow, so check with a professional service technician before installing.

Filters may be located in a number of places in a furnace, depending on the make and model. The diagram at right shows some of the more common locations.

While electric furnaces and heat pumps always have air filters, some gas and oil furnaces do not. If you have a furnace without an air filter, you should install one. Check with a heating system technician if you are unsure how to add a filter.

During the heating season check the air filter every month, and clean or replace it if it appears dirty. Filters typically cost a few dollars at most and are available at hardware stores and home improvement centers.

Have a professional maintain and tune up the furnace ☆ ($, PRO)

Hire a professional service technician periodically to check thermostat operation; clean, adjust, and lubricate moving parts; tighten electrical connections and inspect electrical parts; check fuel connections; test the combustion efficiency; and inspect controls and the starting function. How often you should have professional service depends on how much your heating system operates. For homes in colder regions, annual service is recommended. Heating systems in warm regions should be serviced every 2 to 3 years. In hotter regions, every 3 to 5 years is enough.

Replace the furnace ($$$, PRO)

Furnaces are expensive, but are candidates for replacement if they're worn out, inefficient, or bigger than your house needs. (An oversized furnace can use a lot more power or fuel than a properly-sized one.) Some indicators that you will be better off with a new furnace are:

- The furnace is over 25 years old.
- The furnace combustion efficiency, as tested by a service technician, is lower than 65 percent.
- The heat exchanger is cracked, which you or a service technician may notice during cleaning or inspection.
- Repair or modification would cost more than half as much as replacement.

⚠ *Vent kerosene and gas heaters.* Unvented kerosene and gas heaters should be avoided. Kerosene heaters can be a fire hazard, and both kerosene and gas heaters introduce water vapor to the home (a byproduct of combustion). If not operating properly, unvented kerosene and gas heaters can release dangerous indoor air pollutants.

ℹ *Look for incentives.* Check with your local electric utility about rebates or tax credits for installing a heat pump.

⚠ *Combustion Furnaces.*
Choose only a sealed
combustion furnace specifically
designed for use in a manufactured
home. Sealed combustion
furnaces draw in the air needed
for combustion directly from the
outside, not from the home itself.

- The furnace does not operate well and can't be fixed.

- You've sealed your home's walls, floor, ceiling (page 29) and ducts (page 13), installed storm windows (page 28), and performed heating system maintenance–and you still can't keep your home warm.

- The pilot light in the furnace burns continuously.

A heating system technician can help you evaluate whether a new furnace is appropriate. As part of this evaluation, the technician should measure the efficiency of the existing furnace.

If you have an electric furnace and high heating bills, then consider replacing it with a heat pump. A heat pump combines heating and cooling functions and, in the heating mode, is far more efficient than electric-resistance heat. The more common air-source heat pumps are appropriate for all but the hottest and coldest climates.

2   IMPROVE COOLING SYSTEM PERFORMANCE

Description

There are two broad categories of air conditioners: individual room units (the kind usually mounted in windows), and central systems. Central air conditioners can be further categorized into split systems, in which the compressor/condenser is located outdoors, while the evaporator is inside the home; and packaged systems, in which the entire unit sits outside with ducts carrying air to and from the house. In either type of central system, chilled air is blown through ducts (located either under the floor or in the attic), and into the living space through registers or grates (see diagrams).

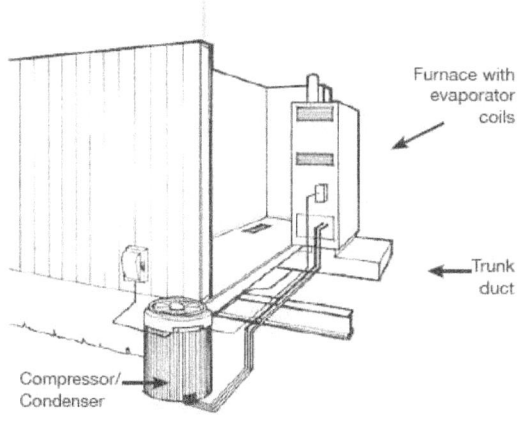

Split system air conditioner

Goal

An efficiently operating cooling system is critical to decreased energy use and increased comfort, particularly in warm climates. A well-maintained air conditioning system will use 15% to 40% less energy than a neglected one. There are several components in cooling systems that need to be properly maintained. Following the tips in this guide will extend the life of your cooling system, and keep it running smoothly and efficiently.

Indicators

If you have central air conditioning or a heat pump and answer YES to any of these questions, cooling system maintenance is especially important for your home:

- Are you in a hot climate?
- Do you find it difficult to keep your home cool in summer?
- Does your cooling system experience frequent breakdowns?

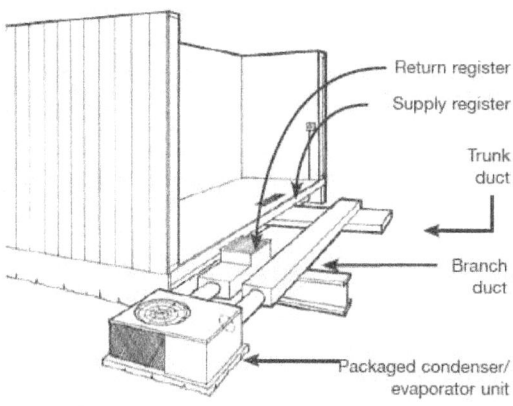

Packaged system air conditioner

Techniques

There are some simple things you can do to make sure your cooling system operates smoothly; other actions require the assistance of a professional. With older and inefficient cooling systems, replacement is often the best option.

Clean or replace the air filter ☆
(FREE or $, low skill)

Air conditioners will have an air filter to prevent dirt from building up on the cooling coils. Examine your unit's filter once a month during the cooling season, and clean or replace it when it appears dirty (which can indicate clogging). This alone can reduce your cooling energy use by 5% to 15%. Many filters are designed to be cleaned, but still may need to be replaced occasionally. This is an easy and inexpensive task that most homeowners can do themselves. Filters in room air conditioners are usually behind the front panel. Most split-system central air conditioners use the furnace's air filter (see page 5, *clean or replace the furnace filter*). In packaged systems, the filter is generally found in the main "return-air" register. The system's user's manual should help you locate it.

⚠ *Inspect duct dampers.*
If you have a packaged system as described on page 9, inspect the duct damper and if necessary, repair or replace it. Air conditioning systems that share ductwork with a furnace must have a damper in the duct. It prevents cool air from entering the furnace cabinet in summer, and warm air from escaping to the air conditioner in winter. A missing or malfunctioning damper can waste tremendous amounts of energy and lead to corrosion of the furnace.

ⓘ *Sizing your air conditioner.*
Bigger is not always better when it comes to your air conditioner. For starters, oversized equipment can be less effective at dehumidifying your house. Not only can this lead to moisture problems in a home, but the higher humidity may force you to lower the thermostat to achieve the same comfort level—increasing your energy use. An oversized unit also cycles on and off more frequently, which increases wear and tear, shortens the service life, increases the frequency of repairs, and reduces efficiency. Plus, it costs more to purchase oversized equipment in the first place. If purchasing a new air conditioner, cooling loads should be carefully calculated by your equipment supplier.

ⓘ *Evaporative coolers.*
If you live in a hot, dry climate, such as the Southwest, an evaporative cooler (swamp cooler) may be a good alternative to a refrigerant-cycle air conditioner. Evaporative coolers use considerably less energy than standard air conditioners. Check with a local air conditioning contractor to find out if such a system makes sense for your home.

Clean the condensing cooling coils
(FREE, medium skill)

Clean the condenser annually by following these simple steps:

1. Turn off the system at the thermostat, if possible, or turn the thermostat up to a setting that will not switch on the air conditioner. Also, turn off the power to the outdoor unit at the main breaker panel or at the disconnect located next to the outdoor unit.

2. Remove any loose debris from around the unit and clean it with gentle household soap and water.

3. Allow the outdoor unit to dry completely before turning on the power at the main breaker panel. After the main power has been restored, turn on the system at the thermostat or set the thermostat for normal operation.

Have a professional perform seasonal maintenance ☆ on central air conditioning systems
($, PRO)

Air conditioner adjustments and repairs should be done by professionals. A professional service technician should clean evaporator and condenser coils, check refrigerant pressures, and adjust and lubricate moving parts. How often you need professional maintenance depends on how much your cooling system operates. For homes in hotter regions (where the air conditioner operates eight or more months per year), annual service is recommended. Cooling systems in warm regions (where the air conditioner operates five to eight months per year) should be serviced every 2 to 3 years. In colder regions (where the air conditioner operates less than five months per year), every 3 to 5 years is usually enough.

Replace the air conditioning system
($$$, PRO)

In some situations it will make sense to replace an older air conditioner with a new, high-efficiency unit. Air conditioner replacement should be considered if the existing unit is worn out, inefficient, or significantly oversized.

Repairing an existing air conditioner may seem to be the least expensive option, but it may cost more in the long run. Paying for repairs on an older, inefficient system may simply prolong the inevitable need for replacement. Installing a new, energy-efficient system may be much more cost-effective.

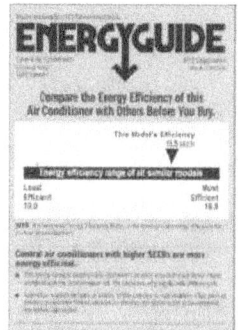

EnergyGuide labels help you identify energy-efficient appliances.

Air conditioner replacement makes sense if:

- The air conditioner is over 10 years old.

- The air conditioner efficiency (SEER or EER) is below 7 or 8.

- Repairs or modifications of an existing unit will cost more than half as much as a replacement.

- The unit does not operate properly and can't be fixed.

- You've sealed your home's walls, floor, ceiling (page 29) and ducts (page 13), installed storm windows (page 28), and performed cooling system maintenance, but still can't keep your home cool.

A cooling system technician can help you evaluate whether a new air conditioning system is appropriate.

Air conditioners have an EnergyGuide label that tells you how much electricity they use based on standard test conditions. Pick one with a low annual energy cost—the smaller the number of kilowatt hours (kWh), the less it will cost to operate. The triangular-shaped arrow should be to the left-of-center on the energy-use line.

Look for ENERGY STAR qualified models, which carry the ENERGY STAR logo on the product or the box. These models are among the most energy-efficient units sold.

If you are going to replace your central air conditioner and you have electric heat in your home, consider replacing the air conditioner with an ENERGY STAR qualified heat pump. A heat pump combines heating and cooling functions and, in the heating mode, is far more efficient than electric-resistance heat. The more common air-source heat pumps are appropriate for all but the coldest and hottest climates.

Dispose of old air conditioners properly. Make sure that they aren't returned to service, and that the refrigerant is properly captured for responsible disposal. Contact your local municipal solid waste agency to make arrangements for disposal.

Other techniques to reduce air conditioner energy cost
(FREE to $, low skill)

Here are a few additional steps you can take to reduce your cooling energy use:

1. Supplement your air conditioner with fans. The air movement will make you feel cooler and allow you to raise the thermostat, reducing air conditioner energy use. Turn off fans, including ceiling fans, when you're not in room—leaving them on wastes energy and actually adds heat. Remember that ENERGY STAR qualified fans are not only energy efficient but also quiet.

2. Nighttime ventilation is another low-cost cooling strategy. If the temperature and humidity drop after the sun goes down, open the windows to exhaust indoor air and pull cool outdoor air into the house.

3. Sunlight on the exterior portion of your air conditioner will reduce its efficiency. Shade the outside components of a central system with trees, shrubs, or a fence and place room units on the north and/or east side of the house. Be sure not to restrict airflow around the unit, however.

Shading an outdoor compressor can improve energy efficiency

3 ELIMINATE LEAKS IN DUCTS

Description

Most manufactured homes have forced-air heating systems. Air from the home is forced through the furnace, where it is warmed by a hot metal heat exchanger or electric heating coils. The warm air is then blown through a system of ducts, and out into each room through registers. In most homes with central air conditioning, the same ducts are used for delivering chilled air during the summer.

The ducts may be in the floor (most common) or in the ceiling (usually only in hotter climates). Typically, each section of a manufactured home has a main trunk duct running its length. Multi-section homes (such as double-wide units) usually have crossover ducts that connect the main trunk ducts. With ceiling-duct systems, the crossover is in the attic and usually inaccessible. In floor-duct systems, the crossover is beneath the home and accessible from the crawlspace (see diagrams).

Leaky ducts are common in older manufactured homes and can dramatically increase heating and cooling bills. It is not uncommon for an older duct system to lose 20% of the heated or chilled air to the outside. If your annual heating and cooling bill is $2,000 and your ducts are leaky, you could be spending $400 every year to heat and cool the outdoors.

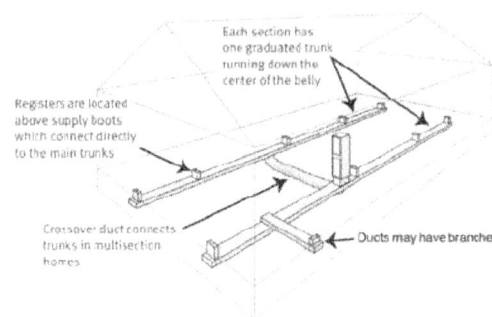

Typical floor duct system

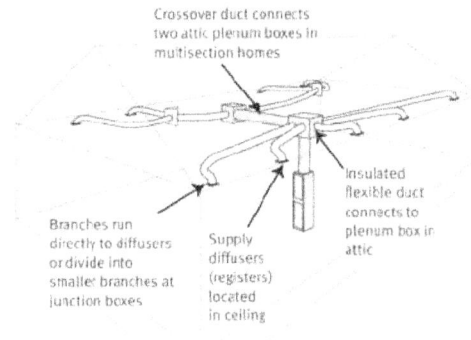

Typical attic duct system

Common duct system leakage locations

Goal

Compared to other energy upgrade measures in a typical manufactured home, sealing the ductwork has one of the largest payoffs relative to its cost. You'll save on your heating and cooling bills, enjoy increased comfort, and reduce the risk of moisture problems.

Indicators

Almost all homes can benefit from duct sealing.
If you answer YES to any of these questions, your home may be especially in need of duct sealing:

- Was your home built before 2000?

- Is the heating and cooling air distribution in your home uneven—that is, do some rooms get a lot of air from the registers, while others don't get enough?

- Is it difficult to heat or cool your home, even after having performed heating and air conditioning system maintenance?

- Does a visual inspection reveal a deteriorated crossover duct (see next page)?

Techniques

Seal the largest leaks first. Duct sealing doesn't require a lot of skill or expensive materials, but you will need time and some dexterity to get at hard-to-reach places. Here's a list of common duct leakage sites, followed by repair suggestions:

Inspecting the duct with a hand-held mirror

Seal supply duct connections to boots and registers ☆
($, medium skill)

Supply ducts can be inspected from inside the home. First remove the registers. You can then inspect the ducts using a mirror and flashlight (see figure). By placing a utility light in one register and looking toward it with a mirror from the next register, you can inspect for leaks and obstructions between those two registers. The main areas to focus on are connections from the main trunk duct to the supply boots that connect to the registers. Other important sites are connections to the branch ducts, furnace, and crossover ducts. Other types of systems that don't use main trunk ducts may require variations on this inspection method.

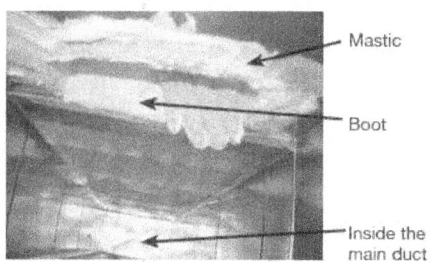

Mastic

Boot

Inside the main duct

Sealing around a register with duct mastic — view from inside the duct

To seal connections from supply boots to registers, follow these steps:

1. Turn off the furnace fan and remove the register grille (there is usually a screw at each end).

2. Clean the duct surfaces (see the box *Duct sealing materials* on page 16).

3. Inspect with a mirror and/or feel the joint between the boot and duct for gaps and tabs that may not be folded tightly against the duct.

4. Fold down any loose tabs and apply reinforcing mesh tape to the corners where the boot meets the duct.

5. Apply mastic (see the box *Duct sealing materials* on page 16).

6. Replace the register grille.

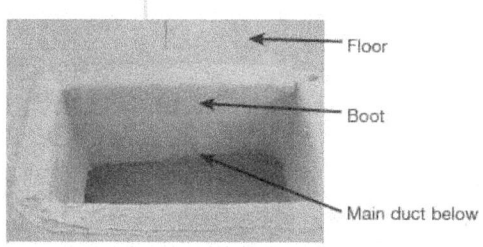

Floor

Boot

Main duct below

Boot sealed with mesh tape and mastic

Seal duct ends ☆
($, medium skill)

The ends of ducts are often major leakage sites. These can be sealed from the inside of the home by cutting a piece of metal flashing to fit the duct and inserting it into the duct from the last register at each end of the duct run. Seal the metal flashing insert with foil tape and mastic.

Make sure all registers are fully open ☆
(FREE, low skill)

Preventing air from flowing out of the registers will make the heating and cooling system less efficient. Make sure registers that have movable louvers are kept in the open position or remove the louvers entirely. Also make sure registers are not covered by rugs or furniture.

Seal and insulate crossover duct and connections ☆
($, high skill)

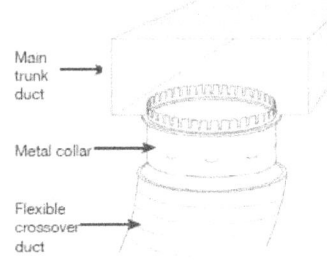

Main trunk duct

Metal collar

Flexible crossover duct

The crossover duct connection must be tightly sealed

Pay particular attention to the crossover duct in multi-section homes. One indicator of a crossover duct leak is if the side of your home where the furnace is located gets a lot more air from the heating and cooling system than the other side. In this case, much of the air going to the second side may be leaking out of the crossover duct into the crawlspace.

Crossover ducts are often insulated flexduct—inner and outer wire-reinforced plastic tubes with fiberglass insulation sandwiched between. The flexduct connects to a metal collar, which in turn connects to the main trunk duct. Both connections should be sealed.

When inspecting the crossover duct, make sure it is firmly connected to the home's rigid duct at both ends, and that there are no gaps, tears or other openings in it. The crossover duct should be supported off the ground with strapping or blocks. Inspect the crossover duct while the furnace fan is running. Feel for air leaking out at all the connections, at each end of the duct, and at any patches.

If the flexduct connection is loose or leaky, re-do the connection by following these steps:

1. Make sure the collar is screwed to the main trunk duct with at least three screws to prevent it from moving or rotating.

2. Seal the collar to the main trunk duct with mastic or foil tape.

3. Apply a ring of duct mastic or putty tape around the collar, and tighten the flexduct's inner ring lining against this sealant. Use a long plastic cable tie as a permanent clamp. Duct mastic will last much longer than putty tape.

4. Seal the inner lining of the flexduct to the collar with duct mastic or aluminum tape.

5. Pull the flexduct's insulation up over the collar, and tape it to the underside of the trunk duct. Cover the tape with mastic.

6. Tighten the outer layer of the flexduct over the collar and use another cable tie to fix it in place.

7. Install three pan-head screws just under the cable tie so the heads of the screws clamp down on the tie.

Fastening the inner lining of the crossover duct to the collar

⚠ Duct tape can be used to hold things together while you create a permanent seal, but use duct mastic, not duct tape, for a long-lasting seal.

Sometimes old ducts are torn or deteriorated. Replace them with new flexduct—preferably with at least R-8 insulation. When replacing a crossover duct, keep it straight and use the minimum length necessary.

Inspect and repair ducts from under the home
($, high skill)

At connections where branch ducts meet the main duct, holes must be sealed from underneath the home. You might have to cut openings in the bottom board to access the ducts. (Don't attempt this unless you're prepared to seal the bottom board back up when you're done!) Working under the home can be difficult and hazardous: wear goggles, gloves, long-sleeved shirts and other protective gear. To locate joints in the duct system, look inside the house for registers that are offset from the main duct. Using exterior walls and windows as reference points, measure to the place where the ducts meet. Use those measurements in the crawlspace to determine just where to cut through the bottom board. Seal these joints with duct mastic, then repair any penetrations through the bottom board. (See *Patch/replace torn or missing bottom board* on page 29.)

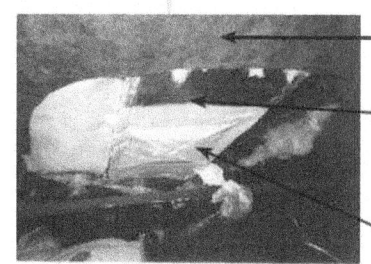

Bottom board

Main duct

Patch sealed with mastic

Duct access hatch sealed with mastic

Seal beneath the furnace
($ materials, high skill to PRO)

This is the area in the duct system with the highest air pressure, so it's the most important place to seal. A metal box, or plenum, typically connects the furnace to the main duct. The seams between the furnace and the plenum, and between the plenum and the main duct, should be carefully sealed.

You can usually access the plenum from underneath the home, following these steps:

1. Cut open the bottom board beneath the furnace and push aside the insulation.

2. Cut an 8 to 10-inch square or rectangular temporary access hatch in the bottom of the duct directly under the furnace—but only cut three sides of the hole, leaving a flap. Through this temporary hatch, you can see the furnace-to-duct connection and can seal any leaks with duct mastic and fiberglass-reinforcing mesh tape. The cut metal will have sharp edges. Line the edges of the hole temporarily with duct tape to prevent injury.

3. Seal the temporary access hatch that you cut into the duct using duct mastic and fiberglass tape, replace the insulation and patch the bottom board. (See *Patch/replace torn or missing bottom board* on page 29.)

Seal cracks closest to furnace fan. Cracks in areas with the highest air pressure (closest to the furnace fan) will leak the most air. Sealing them will have the biggest impact on energy savings.

Do not block louvers or grilles. Air needs a path to get back to the furnace. Never block the louvers or grilles in doors or walls enclosing the furnace.

⚠ *Turn off emergency power.* Whenever working with a furnace, especially an electric furnace, turn off the emergency power switch first.

In some situations, the seams may be accessible from inside the home without removing the furnace. Some furnaces have a bottom cooling coil compartment with a removable panel. If the furnace has such a compartment, but doesn't have a cooling coil, it provides a way to access the main duct beneath the furnace. Also, the heating coils in an electric furnace can be taken out to provide access to the duct—though this is a difficult and potentially hazardous job that should only be attempted by a skilled technician. Similarly, the entire furnace itself can be temporarily removed to seal leaks, but this too is a job best left to professionals.

Duct sealing materials

Thoroughly clean the duct first with a solvent or steel wool before patching. To seal, do not use duct tape. Before long, the adhesive will fail and the tape will fall off. Recommended materials are:

- **Silicone caulk** is excellent for sealing small holes and narrow cracks. It is widely available at home improvement centers.

- **Aluminum-foil-faced butyl tape** is available from heating and cooling wholesalers. Use only UL181A foil tape for metal ducts or UL131B for non-metallic ducts. It is good for large holes and cracks, especially in corners. If possible, install tape on the inside of ducts, because air pressure may eventually push it off if it's on the outside. Clean and dry surfaces well and tightly stretch the tape over the duct. For a longer-lasting seal, secure the tape with staples (into wood) or mastic (on metal).

- **Acrylic duct mastic**, a thin putty available from heating and cooling equipment suppliers and mail- order suppliers of weatherization materials. This is the best duct-sealing material. It can be installed with a brush, spatula, or your fingers if you wear rubber gloves. For larger openings or gaps, use fiberglass mesh tape to reinforce the duct mastic. Special tape designed for mastic is available or you can use standard gypsum wall board tape. The finished coat of mastic should be about 1/8" inch thick and you should not be able to see the seam through the mastic coat.

4 IMPROVE LIGHTING EFFICIENCY

Description

Lighting is responsible for about 12% of the energy used in a typical American home.

Goal

Nearly every home can benefit from improved lighting efficiency. No matter the type of lighting in your home, there are opportunities to lower your monthly energy costs by reducing your electricity use. You can also improve the quality of light at the same time.

Indicators

The average home has nine lights left on for more than three hours every day. Any light bulb burning more than two hours per day on average is a good candidate to be replaced with a compact fluorescent lamp (CFL).

Techniques

These simple techniques to lower lighting costs and improve lighting quality can be done with little or no skill and low cost:

Compact fluorescent lamp

Replace incandescent light bulbs with compact fluorescents ($, low skill)

CFLs use one-third to one-quarter the energy of incandescent bulbs, and last up to ten times longer. They screw into standard light bulb sockets, and are available in many sizes and shapes to fit almost any fixture. They're more expensive to buy than incandescent bulbs, but save several times their purchase cost because of reduced electric use and longer life (less frequent replacement).

The packaging for a CFL usually indicates the equivalent wattage of the incandescent bulb it replaces. For example, a 20-watt CFL gives off about the same amount of light as a 75-watt incandescent bulb. Note that CFLs take up to a minute to reach full brightness.

Look for ENERGY STAR qualified models, which carry the ENERGY STAR logo on the product or the box. These models are among the most energy-efficient units sold.

Example of savings from a compact fluorescent bulb

If you replace one 75-watt incandescent bulb (that costs 75¢ and is on for four hours per day) with a 20-watt compact fluorescent lamp (that costs $5 and is also on for four hours per day), you'll save about $3 by the end of the first year, and more than $50 over the expected seven-year life of the CFL.

ⓘ *Turn lights off.*
The lamp that uses the least energy is the one that's switched off. Turn off the lights when you don't need them.

Install energy-saving controls on exterior lights
($, medium skill)

Outdoor lighting should be off when it's not needed. Photocell switches can automate lights by shutting them off when the sun comes up. Timers can automatically turn off outdoor lights in the evening, such as patio lights that are no longer needed when you go indoors. Motion sensors can turn on lights when they detect movement. These devices are available at hardware stores and home improvement centers for as little as $15. Hard-wired fixtures may require an electrician.

Clean fixtures
(FREE, low skill)

Keep lamps, lampshades and light bulbs clean to maximize their light output.
You may even find that once a fixture is clean, it gives off the same amount of light as a higher-wattage bulb.

Use low-wattage light bulbs
($, low skill)

In some fixtures, it's possible to use lower-wattage light bulbs and still get the amount of light you need.

5 IMPROVE REFRIGERATOR PERFORMANCE

Description

Refrigerators account for about one-sixth of the typical electric bill for an American home and 9% of the total energy used in manufactured homes. Old, inefficient models are good candidates for replacement.

Goal

Today's refrigerators use 40% less electricity than 20-year-old models. An old, inefficient refrigerator can cost up to $280 a year to run; a new, efficient refrigerator can save more than $150 each year over a 20-year-old model. While the savings will be less if replacing a newer refrigerator, it still will save between $35 and $70 per year. That's $525 to $1,050 during the 15-year typical lifespan of a refrigerator.

Indicators

You should consider replacing your refrigerator if:

- The one you have now is more than 15 years old.
- Your refrigerator is not keeping food cold or is especially noisy.

Techniques

Replacing the refrigerator can generate the greatest savings, but other techniques can also improve the performance of your existing unit.

Operate your existing refrigerator properly
(FREE, low skill)

If you decide not to replace your refrigerator, these tips can help save money with your existing one:

- If the refrigerator is in direct sunlight or near an oven, dishwasher, or other heat source, it has to work harder to stay cool. Relocate it if possible, or shield it from excess heat.
- If the door seals aren't airtight (they won't hold a dollar bill snugly when closed) or if condensation forms around the door seals, replace them.
- The proper temperature for refrigerators is between 37° and 40° Fahrenheit; freezers should be between 0° to 5°. A refrigerator that's 10° cooler than it needs to be can use 25% more energy.
- Defrost manual-defrost models regularly. Less energy is needed when there's no frost buildup.
- Make sure that air can circulate freely behind the refrigerator, or wherever the coils are located. Air flow is required to carry heat away.
- Periodically vacuum or brush the coils to improve efficiency. Refrigerator coil brushes are available at most hardware stores.

Dispose of old refrigerators

Old refrigerators are energy hogs that may cost as much as $280 a year to run. Keeping one around as a second fridge is an expensive proposition. See if your local energy utility offers refrigerator recycling incentives and disposal programs, or contact your local municipal solid waste agency to make arrangements for disposal.

Buy a new refrigerator
($$-$$$, low skill)

Refrigerators have an EnergyGuide label that tells you how much electricity they use based on standard test conditions. Pick one with a low annual energy cost—the smaller the number of kilowatt hours (kWh), the less it will cost to operate. The triangular-shaped arrow should be to the left-of-center on the energy-use line.

Look for ENERGY STAR qualified models, which carry the ENERGY STAR logo on the product or the box. These models are among the most energy-efficient units sold.

Check with your local utility to see if they offer rebates on new energy-efficient models, or recycling incentives for older models.

Other buying tips

- Refrigerator-freezers that have the freezer compartment on the top or the bottom are generally more energy efficient than side-by-side models of a similar size.

- Through-the-wall ice makers use a lot of energy.

- A refrigerator that's bigger than you need can waste energy and space. One that's smaller than you need can mean extra driving for groceries. Carefully consider what size is best for you. A full refrigerator uses less energy than an empty one.

6 IMPROVE WATER HEATER PERFORMANCE

Description

Most manufactured homes have conventional storage-tank water heaters located in closets. Older manufactured homes sometimes have smaller water heaters in kitchen cabinets instead. Electric and gas-fired water heaters are the most common.

Goal

Water heating accounts for about 15% of energy costs in a typical manufactured home. Improving the energy efficiency of the water heater can save a significant amount of money over the water heater's lifetime.

Indicators

Nearly every home can benefit from water heater maintenance and efficiency improvements. The more hot water your family uses, the greater the opportunities for savings.

Techniques

There are a number of simple actions you can take to reduce your water heating costs.

Insulate the tank ☆
($, medium skill)

Insulating an electric water heater is one of the most effective and least expensive energy-saving steps you can take, saving more than enough money in one year to pay for the cost of the materials. After that, the savings go in your pocket.

Insulation jackets for water heaters usually cost $20 or less at home centers. Follow the installation instructions that come with the jacket. Alternatively, standard fiberglass batt insulation can be used. Seal the seams with vinyl tape, and wrap the entire heater loosely with wire ties to hold the insulation in place.

No matter how you choose to insulate the water heater, pay close attention to these safety instructions:

- Cover the sides and top of the heater, but cut flaps for the electric element access panels and the thermostat.

- Do not cover warning labels on the tank.

- Do not insulate gas or oil fired water heater tanks. Over time, the insulation may sag, blocking air intakes and creating a safety hazard.

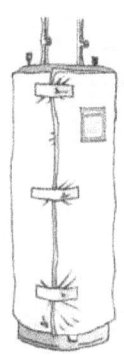

Water heater with insulation jacket

Fix Those Leaks!

Leaky faucets and showerheads can waste huge amounts of water—and energy—if hot water is leaking. A leak that produces one drop per second will waste over 190 gallons per month, or 2,300 gallons per year. A leak that fills an 8-ounce cup in a minute will waste 2,700 gallons per month and 33,000 gallons per year—enough to fill a swimming pool!

⚠ *Shut off power.*
Before attempting any work on your electric water heater, make sure the power to it is shut off at the circuit breaker.

⚠ *Take safety precautions.*
Important safety precautions must be taken when insulating a water heater. See the precautions listed at left.

⚠ *Finding the right temperature.*
If the water heater temperature isn't high enough, there are some circumstances in which Legionella bacteria can grow—the cause of Legionnaires' disease. Although 120° is usually considered hot enough to prevent this, homeowners at high risk of susceptibility (such as transplant patients and smokers with chronic lung conditions) may be advised to keep their water heater settings higher (140°). Check with a physician if uncertain.

🛈 *When you're away.*
If you'll be away for an extended period, turn the thermostat to the lowest possible setting—or turn the water heater off completely. Make sure you know how to relight the pilot light if your gas heater has one.

⚠ *Turn the power off.*
Make sure the power is off to electric heaters before draining the tank. Exposing the electric elements to the air with the power on may cause them to burn out.

⚠ *Service the unit.*
Older tanks that have never been cleaned will often require additional procedures. Check with a service technician.

Insulate water pipes leading from the tank ☆

Insulating the water pipes slows heat loss. It also raises the temperature of hot water at the tap by 2° to 4°, which lets you lower the temperature setting on the water heater. Pipe insulation is usually a foam sleeve, slit lengthwise, that costs less than 50¢ per foot at home centers. Insulate all of the hot water piping that is accessible. It is especially important to insulate the first six feet of pipe coming out of the water heater. Fasten the insulation sleeve with electrical tape, wire or cable ties at least once per foot. For a snug fit, choose pipe insulation whose inside diameter is the same as the outside diameter of the pipe. Miter-cut corners and tape them closed. Insulating cold water pipes is also beneficial, especially in humid climates. It will reduce sweating in summer—a problem than can cause moisture damage.

Lower the water heater thermostat ☆
(FREE, low skill)

For every 10° you turn down the water heater, you'll save about 3% to 5% on water heating costs. A setting of 120° (usually halfway between "low" and "medium") is usually hot enough. If you have a dishwasher without booster heat, set the thermostat at 140° (typically "medium"). Some electric water heaters have two thermostats—one for each element. Adjust both to the same setting. Another benefit of lowering the thermostat is that it reduces the risk of children scalding themselves in the kitchen or bath. You can check the temperature of your water at the taps by continually running hot water in cup with a thermometer placed in it.

Clean the tank
(FREE, medium skill)

Once a year, drain a gallon of water through the spigot at the bottom of the water heater to remove sediment, which decreases its energy efficiency—and can, in some situations, provide a more protected environment for Legionella bacteria to grow.

Install low-flow showerheads and faucet aerators
($, low skill)

If your showerhead was manufactured before 1995, it may use as much as 5 or 7 gallons per minute, wasting a tremendous amount of hot water. Replacing it with a high-quality new one that uses no more than 2.5 gallons per minute will probably pay for itself in a matter of months—and you'll be far less likely to run out of hot water. In many homes, the existing showerhead can be unscrewed and a new one installed. You'll need a pipe wrench and Teflon® tape. Protect the finish with a rag while you work.

Low-flow aerators also reduce water use. They screw into standard faucets to reduce the flow and aerate the water, so that it still feels like a full flow. These cost just a dollar or two, and can pay back the expense in just a few months.

Replace your water heater
($$, PRO)

If warranted, replace the water heater with a new, more efficient unit. If a water heater was manufactured before 1980, it may be cost-effective to replace it with a more efficient model. Always check the EnergyGuide label to determine the unit's energy efficiency.

7 REDUCE SOLAR HEAT

Description

Sunlight coming in through the windows is a major contributor to cooling bills in many areas of the country. Trees and other foliage can be very effective in shading a home, but there are other relatively simple options available to reduce the heat while maintaining views. Blocking sunlight has other benefits, including less fading of furniture and carpets, more comfortable temperatures in rooms with large windows, and less glare.

Goal

Following these tips will reduce the cost of cooling your home and make it more comfortable during the hottest parts of the day.

Indicators

If you answer YES to any of these questions, you should consider ways to reduce your home's solar gain:

- Are you in a hot climate?
- Do you find it difficult to keep your home cool in summer, especially during mid-day and early afternoon, despite having a properly maintained cooling system?
- Do you have large windows facing west or east that receive direct sunlight in summer?

Techniques

There are some simple actions you can take to reduce the impact the sun has on your cooling costs.

Install sun screens
($$, high skill)

Sun screens are often the least expensive window-shading option that retains a full view through the window. Typical sun screens absorb more than a third of the sunlight's heat. Most can be removed in winter when you may need the extra heat. Like regular window screens, sun screens have aluminum frames and are installed on the exterior side of the windows. They're available in several colors and are often used to shade porches. Making an effective sun screen is difficult. You may wish to use a sun screen kit instead. Having a professional build and install custom sun screens should cost about $2 to $4 per square foot.

Also consider plantings for shade

Planting trees or shrubs can provide very effective shade. Deciduous trees (which loose their leaves in winter) provide shade in summer but allow solar heat in during the colder months. Taller trees without low branches on the south side will block the higher summer sun without blocking views. Smaller trees or shrubs on the east and west will block the lower summer sun, but they also impact views. If permanent plantings aren't permitted or are impractical, vines on a temporary trellis and tall annuals can provide excellent shading. Consider clematis, morning glory, and sunflowers.

Install exterior awnings
($$-$$$, medium skill)

Awnings are expensive but popular in hot, sunny climates. They intercept solar heat before it gets to the window, which reduces the energy needed for cooling. When selecting awnings, consider:

- How much shade do you want? This is affected by how low the bottom of the awing extends (called the drop) and how far it sticks out.

- How important is it to maintain a view out the window?

- How much will an awning cost? Do-it-yourself kits and store-bought (manufactured) awnings are less expensive than custom-made ones.

On the south side of the house, the drop should be 45% to 60% of the window height. Awnings on the east and west sides need to extend lower to block the morning or afternoon sun, which is low in the sky. These should have a drop of 60% to 75%. Awnings without sides will work better if they're wider than the windows.

Metal awning

Apply reflective window film
($$, high skill)

Fabric awning with sides

Metallized plastic window films can block half to three-quarters of the sunlight's heat and glare and prevent almost all of the ultraviolet rays from coming through the window. These films can lower your cooling bills in summer, but actually raise heating bills in winter, so they are generally more beneficial in hotter climates. The reflective film is installed on the inside of the window and makes the window more reflective when viewed from outside. Note that these reflective window films block daylight in addition to solar heat—though newer "low-e" films let through more visible light while stopping most of the heat. Reflective window films are difficult to work with, making for a potentially frustrating do-it-yourself project. Professional installation will cost about $3 per square foot. Low-quality reflective films can become cloudy or start to deteriorate after just a few years; high-quality ones last longer and have scratch-resistant coatings.

Don't confuse reflective window films with tinted films that color the glass. Those films absorb rather than reflect heat, so they're not as effective in preventing solar heat from entering the home. They can actually heat the glass to high enough temperatures to cause damage.

Use interior shades to block sunlight from entering the home
($$, medium skill)

Window shades and blinds with metallized or bright white reflective surfaces can effectively block solar heat. The following table describes some options available at many window treatment retailers:

Table 4

Type	Solar heat	View and light
Opaque roller shades with white surfaces facing the exterior	Reduces solar gain by about 80%	No view or light when the shades are drawn.
Roller shades with metallized plastic window film	Reduces solar gain by about 50%-75%	Preserves the view and lets in some light
White Venetian blinds	Reduces solar gain by about 40%-60%	Blocks most of the view and light

Install a reflective roof coating
($$$, PRO)

A great deal of unwanted heat gain enters a home through the roof—the less insulation, the more summertime heat gain. White roof coatings are available for metal, asphalt shingle and other types of roofs. These coatings will reflect more than 75% of the sunlight striking the roof. Most are acrylic and relatively easy to apply, although they do require working on top of the roof. They have the added benefit of fixing small leaks in the roof and extending its life. Light-colored roofs should be cleaned each year to keep them reflective.

8   IMPROVE WINDOW PERFORMANCE

Description

Storm windows can be installed over existing windows to improve their insulation value and dramatically reduce air leakage and drafts. Separate, removable storm windows can be installed in seasons when heating or cooling is typically necessary (and the windows don't need to be opened), and removed during more temperate seasons or if windows need to be operable for ventilation. Storm windows are most needed in cold climates, and less important in warmer regions. Triple-track storm windows, mounted outside the primary windows, open and close easily and provide screens, but they are quite expensive and generally must be installed by professionals. Interior storm windows have been found to work best for manufactured homes, and only these will be addressed here.

Not all storm windows will work on manufactured homes because of the way windows are installed. Be sure you select windows suitable for your home.

Interior storm window with flexible plastic glazing

Goal

Following these tips will reduce the cost of heating your home and make it more comfortable during the coldest times of the year.

Indicators

If you answer YES to any of these questions, you should consider adding storm windows:

- Are you in a colder climate?

- Was your home built before 1976, and does it have the original windows? (After 1976, manufacturers were required to provide homes with either double-pane windows or storm windows in many parts of the country.)

- Was your home built after 1976, but the original storm windows are lost or broken (and your primary windows are single-pane)?

- Do you have jalousie windows?

- Do the windows feel uncomfortably cold in winter, and you notice drafts coming through them?

- Do your heating bills seem excessive?

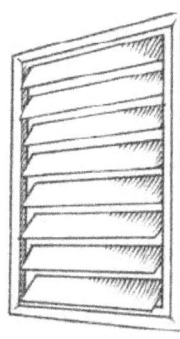

Jalousie windows with louvered pieces of glass are notoriously leaky and should be replaced.

⚠ *Jalousie and awning windows.*
Old jalousie and awning
windows require special storm
window frames with holes to
accommodate the protruding
cranks, or the cranks can be
removed when the storms
are installed.

⚠ *Fire escapes.*
Don't install a fixed storm window
over a fire escape window without
making sure that everyone living
in the home can quickly and easily
remove it.

Techniques

There are a number of options for adding storm windows to manufactured homes.

Install interior storm windows ☆
($$-$$$, medium to high skill)

A number of different types of interior storm windows are available for different budgets and primary window types. Storm windows are available from home improvement centers as kits or already assembled. The kits are designed to be installed by homeowners with a minimum of experience and tools. Preassembled storm windows usually require more skill and equipment.

Interior storm windows can be fixed or sliding. Fixed storm windows are removed seasonally. Either the entire panel is removed, or the sash is removed and a frame remains behind. The bottom of a fixed storm window should be supported by a sill, clip, or on a wood or aluminum strip to support the window's weight. Because they are removed seasonally, they can be lost or damaged. For the handy do-it-yourselfer, fixed storm windows can be made from wood frames and plastic sheeting.

Sliding storm windows are more expensive than fixed ones. They usually have aluminum or vinyl frames and a spring loaded latch. Their primary advantage is that they can be left on all year long and opened for ventilation. They're compatible with vertical or horizontal sliding primary windows.

Often a combination of fixed and sliding storm windows is the best solution, with the sliding windows being used for ventilation and emergency exit requirements.

When considering window material, the choice is either glass or plastic. Plastic glazing costs less than glass. It's also lighter, which is a big benefit for removable storm windows. Both rigid plastics (acrylic and polycarbonate) and flexible plastics (vinyl, polyester, and polyethylene) are available. Each material has advantages and disadvantages. For example, acrylic is prone to scratching; polycarbonate may yellow over time; and thinner, flexible plastics may tear.

Whatever type of storm window you choose, the frame should seal tightly and continuously against the interior wall or window trim using foam, foam tape, magnetic seal, or other method.

Install plastic disposable window insulating kits
($, low skill)

These plastic kits, available at home improvement centers and other retail outlets, are designed to be applied over the primary windows for seasonal use. They install with double-sided tape and shrink to fit with heat from a hair dryer. Effective at reducing air leakage through cracks around windows and patio doors, these kits are a low-cost alternative to storm windows, but they can only be used once.

9 ELIMINATE LEAKS IN THE WALLS, FLOOR AND CEILING

Description

Air leaking through the walls, floors, and ceilings of your home can have a significant impact on your heating and cooling bills, as well as your comfort. It can also contribute to moisture-related problems. While windows and doors are common sources of air leaks, more important leakage sites are often in less visible places. (Leaks in the ducts are also very important to seal. See page 12.)

Goal

Following these tips will reduce the unwanted exchange of warm and cold air through your home's walls, floor, and ceiling, which will in turn result in lower heating and cooling bills. It will also make your home a lot more comfortable by reducing drafts.

Indicators

Almost all homes can benefit from air sealing. If you answer YES to any of these questions, your home may be especially in need of sealing:

- Is your home more than 10 years old?
- Do you frequently feel drafts on windy days?
- In winter, is the air near the floor more than about 5° cooler than the air near the ceiling?
- Is it difficult to heat or cool your home—even after having performed heating system (page 6) and air conditioning system (page 9) maintenance?

Techniques

In general, large openings should be tackled first, then smaller ones, and finally the little holes and cracks. Most of these techniques do not require skill or expensive materials, but they will require time and care. Descriptions of common leakage sites—listed in order of importance—follow, along with repair suggestions.

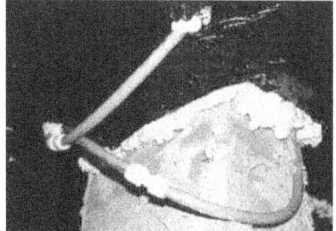

Bottom board penetrations sealed with patch and foam

Patch/replace torn or missing bottom board ☆
($, medium skill)

The bottom board (also called the belly or underbelly) is the protective covering on the bottom of the home. If torn, it can be a major source of air leakage, which will drive up energy costs—and a potential source of moisture problems. Patching the bottom board with durable materials designed for that purpose is the best way to reduce this type of energy loss.

Bottom boards consist of either a flexible or rigid material. If you have a flexible bottom board made of paper or fabric, use similar material for a patch, or purchase special patching material from a manufactured home supply retailer. A combination of adhesives, foam and fasteners works best for producing a long-lasting, airtight seal. When possible, fasten patches to the floor joists with staples, nails, or screws. If no backing is available, you can use construction adhesive to glue the patch to the bottom board.

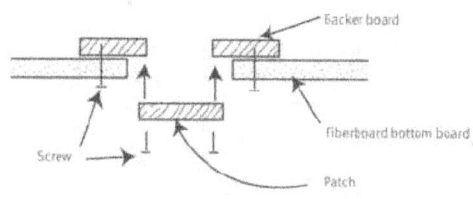

Patching a rigid bottom board

As you reduce air leakage through your home's walls, floor and ceiling, take steps to avoid moisture problems. This is especially true in hot, humid climates for homes that are air conditioned. The following tips are useful for all homes:

- Make sure the ground is sloped in all directions to drain rain water away from the home.

- Ensure that kitchen and bathroom exhaust fans are operable and used regularly. Bath fans should be wired to the light switch and operate when the light is on.

- Make sure that clothes dryer vents are unobstructed and exhaust directly to the outside, and are not vented to the crawlspace under the home.

- Install and periodically clean rain gutters; use a downspout and extension to direct water away from the home.

- Maintain or install a 6-mil plastic vapor barrier on the entire ground surface under the home.

⚠ *Sealing walls.*
The most important surface to seal in manufactured homes is the interior wall surface. The exterior wall surface is designed as a weather barrier to prevent rain from leaking in. This surface is often is designed to be vented, so if water gets into the wall, it can dry to the exterior. Don't seal the walls from the exterior except to stop water from leaking in.

A variety of materials are used for rigid bottom boards, including plywood, paneling, and rigid insulation. To patch a rigid bottom board, cut a rectangle around the damaged part and remove it. Then insert one or more pieces of wood or plywood (backer board), large enough to overlap the empty rectangular hole. Drive screws up through the bottom board and into this backer board to hold it tightly in place. This provides something rigid to secure the patch to. Cut a patch slightly smaller than the opening, and fasten it to the backer board with screws. Then caulk the joint around the patch, providing a good seal to the original bottom board.

Seal gaps and cracks in the walls, floor and ceiling
($, medium skill)

To seal large openings, use a piece of material that is the same as or similar to the surface being patched. To cover a hole in a concealed area, such as behind a washing machine, cut a patch that overlaps the opening by a few inches on all sides. Apply adhesive around the opening, and press the patch into place. Use screws or nails if necessary. Then use caulk or expanding foam to seal remaining air leaks such as around a pipe, flue, or wiring that passes through the patch.

Hole in floor at plumbing penetration behind tub

Caulk works well for small cracks. Openings more than about a quarter-inch wide should be stuffed with foam rubber backer rod or some other compressible material, and then caulked or sealed with expanding foam.

For most indoor applications, a good quality latex caulk is satisfactory. It's inexpensive, easy to apply, paintable, and cleans up with water.
For exterior applications, more expensive silicone or polyurethane caulk will perform better. Areas that are exposed to heated surfaces such as around flues should be sealed with a caulk specially formulated for high temperatures.

Urethane foam sealant, available in a can, is excellent for sealing small to medium-sized openings in a wide variety of locations, including the bottom board.

Some common leakage sites include:

- Openings between the furnace closet and the attic and/or floor cavity.

- Plumbing penetrations where pipes enter exterior walls, or between exterior (unheated) water heater closets and adjoining rooms. Look under sinks, behind and under bathtubs, in back of washing machines, and around hose bibs and outdoor faucets.

- Penetrations for electrical outlets, service panels and light fixtures.

- Around flue and vent pipe penetrations and exhaust fans.

- Openings from closets and cabinets into walls, floors or attic.

Cover window air conditioners
($, low skill)

If left in place during the winter months, window air conditioners can result in significant air leakage through the unit. Interior and exterior covers, available at home improvement centers, can reduce this leakage. Or the units can be removed and the windows closed and weatherized. Seal all gaps around window air conditioners.

Seal leaky windows—particularly if they do not close properly
($, low skill)

Weatherstripping or caulk can be used to seal cracks and gaps around window frames. Alternatively, do-it-yourself plastic window insulating kits, available at hardware stores, can reduce winter drafts coming from leaky windows. A more expensive option that also improves window insulation is to install storm windows (see page 28).

Windows should be repaired if they no longer operate properly or if glass is broken. A contractor can help with this task. Replacing windows with more efficient models is generally not cost effective unless the windows are damaged and need to be replaced anyway.

When replacing windows, look for ENERGY STAR qualified models, which carry the ENERGY STAR logo on the product or the box. These models are among the most energy-efficient units sold.

Fix poorly fitting exterior doors
($, medium skill)

If the door itself is in good shape but air leaks in around the edges, weatherstripping may be the answer. The first thing to check is whether door opens in or out.

Doors that swing out usually have weatherstripping attached in a track on the door frame, but sometimes on the door itself. The weatherstripping on these doors is typically a vinyl flap. The vinyl flap can be replaced, or you can add silicone tube weatherstripping to it.

Doors that open in are weatherstripped the same way as doors on site-built homes. Just follow the instructions on the packaging for the weatherstripping product you select.

When shopping for weatherstripping look for flexibility and longevity. Silicone rubber, neoprene rubber, and plastic-jacketed foam rubber are recommended. Vinyl tubing, felt and foam tapes generally will not perform as well or last as long.

If the door is so badly damaged that it needs to be replaced, look for ENERGY STAR qualified models, which carry the ENERGY STAR logo on the product or the box. These models are among the most energy-efficient units sold.

⚠ *Sealing windows.*
Pay special attention to sealing jalousie and older crank-out awning windows, as these are often especially leaky.

10 INSULATE THE WALLS, FLOORS, AND CEILING

❶ *Add plastic sheeting.*
Prevent rising damp by laying plastic sheeting on the bottom of the crawlspace. This can prevent condensation from making the insulation wet, which reduces its performance, and helps avoid moisture problems.

Description

Insulation in walls, floors, and ceilings acts like a blanket, keeping the heat inside your home in winter—and keeping the heat out of your air-conditioned home in summer. Like a blanket, the thicker the insulation, the better it works. The performance level of insulation is called its R-value, which indicates its resistance to heat flow. (As R-value goes up, energy use goes down).

Insulation in manufactured home walls and floors is usually fiberglass batts. Ceiling insulation is usually loose-fill fiberglass or cellulose. Before the first energy crisis in 1973, most homes built in the U.S.—including manufactured homes—contained little insulation. The level of insulation used in homes has been increasing ever since. The recommended amount of insulation for a given house depends on its climate; colder climates generally demand more insulation.

Goal

Determine if your home is a candidate for adding insulation. Decide what part of your home, if any, should be insulated: floor, ceiling and/or walls.

Indicators

Many manufactured homes can benefit from additional insulation. If you answer YES to any of these questions, your home may be a candidate:

- Was your home built before 1994? (That year, stricter insulation standards went into effect.) If your home was built before 1976 and has never been upgraded, then it can almost certainly benefit from more insulation.

- Is it difficult to heat or cool your home—even after having performed heating system (page 6) and air conditioning system (page 9) maintenance, and sealing air leaks in the ducts (page 12), walls, floor and ceiling (page 29)?

- In colder climates, are the walls cool to the touch in winter?

- During the winter, is the air near the floor of your home at least 5° cooler than the air near the ceiling, and is the house drafty?

- Using the techniques described in the box *Measure your existing insulation level* on page 34, is your home significantly underinsulated—and is there room for more insulation to be added to your floor, ceiling and/or walls?

Techniques

In general, adding insulation to the floor is the most cost-effective approach with manufactured homes, followed by adding insulation to the ceiling. The amount of insulation that can be cost-effectively added to wall, floor, or ceiling cavities depends on the amount of insulation already there, how much empty space remains, and your local climate and fuel costs.

Adding insulation to a manufactured home is almost always best done by professionals since specialized equipment is usually required and incorrect installation can damage the home.

The following descriptions will give you an idea of what a professional contractor will do when upgrades are performed.

Add insulation to the floor
($$$, PRO)

Floors in older manufactured homes can lose a lot of heat in cool climates
due to relatively low levels of insulation. Floors can also be a big source of air leakage
which wastes energy and can cause moisture problems. Floor insulation is commonly
added to manufactured homes by blowing loose fiberglass wool through a hose into
holes cut in the bottom board. The holes should be sealed with a durable patch (see
page 29) after the insulation is added. Alternatively, insulation may be added through
a fill-tube inserted into holes cut in the home's rim joists. Take care not to damage the
joists' structural integrity. These holes should also be patched.

Add insulation to the roof
($$$, PRO)

Adding insulation to roof cavities is cost effective in most climates for manufactured
homes that don't have adequate ceiling insulation. The primary benefit is reduced winter
heating loads, but it also reduces summer cooling costs. Typically, roof cavity (ceiling)
insulation is blown in through holes in the ceiling, holes in the roof, or holes through the
raised edge of a home's metal roof. If insulation is added through the ceiling, holes will
need to be drilled between each roof truss, and in each half of double-section homes.
The holes should be patched afterward with gypsum board, plastic plugs or trim board.
If blown through the roof, the roof must be repaired afterward to prevent water leakage.
Insulation can also be blown in from the end of the home with a long pipe. Before adding
insulation to the roof cavity, the ceiling should be sealed against air leakage to prevent
insulation dust and fibers from blowing into the living area.

Another method of adding roof insulation to manufactured homes with unvented metal
roofs is to install rigid insulation boards right on top of the existing roof, then installing
new waterproof roofing on top of the insulation. This is a more expensive option and it
should be done in conjunction with blowing insulation into the roof cavity to maximize
effectiveness. Before selecting this option, the contractor must make sure the attic
cavity is tightly sealed against air infiltration. A leaky attic will negate much of the
benefit of added roof insulation.

⚠ *Adding roof insulation.*
When adding roof-cavity insulation,
the contractor must take care to
maintain clearances between the
insulation and recessed ceiling
light fixtures and flues to avoid
overheating; make sure the ceiling
is strong enough to support the
weight of the additional insulation;
and not block ventilation in
vented attics.

ⓘ *Avoid insulated skirting.*
Since the space under the home
must be vented, insulated skirting
generally is not an effective
strategy to save energy.

Blowing insulation into the floor cavity

Blowing insulation into the roof

Add insulation to sidewalls
($$$, PRO)

The walls of older manufactured homes may have significant voids where insulation is missing. Adding wall insulation is difficult and expensive, but it can be cost-effective in colder climates that have high fuel costs. There are at least four different ways to add insulation to walls: blowing insulation through holes drilled in the exterior siding; blowing insulation through holes drilled in the interior wall; installing fiberglass batts after removing the exterior siding; and stuffing fiberglass batts into walls from below. All of these techniques are difficult and expensive. On some homes, several different methods might be combined because of variations in the walls' construction.

Measure your existing insulation level

Homes in colder climates should have a minimum of R-11 in the walls and R-21 in the floor and ceiling if it will fit. Each inch of fiberglass-batt insulation provides an insulating value of about R-3.2, and every inch of loose-fill fiberglass provides about R-2.5. For example, a wall with 3-1/2" fiberglass-batt insulation achieves about R-11.

Figuring out how much insulation there is in your home can be tricky. For walls, you can sometimes remove the cover plate from an electrical outlet (turning off power at your circuit breaker first) and look into the gap next to the outlet box. For floors, you may be able to remove a floor-mounted heating register. For your ceiling, removing a recessed light fixture, electrical cover plate from a ceiling-hung light fixture, or bathroom fan cover plate may reveal the insulation. In a hidden location such as a closet or cabinet, you can cut a hole into the wall, floor, or ceiling cavity.

One important limiting factor in being able to add insulation to your home may be the thickness of the wall, floor, or roof cavity. If your floor cavity is only 6" deep, you'll only be able to achieve about R-15 with loose-fill insulation.

ⓘ LIFESTYLE TIPS TO SAVE ENERGY

Here are several common-sense, low-cost or no-cost strategies that you can implement today to lower your energy bills.

During the cooling season:

1. Close drapes or shades on the sunny side of the house to reduce solar heat through the windows.

2. Set the thermostat to 78°F or higher. When the house is empty, set it to 82°F or higher.

3. Turn off the air conditioner when nobody's home, or when cooling isn't needed. If conditions permit, open windows for ventilation instead of using the air conditioner. However, in very humid conditions, opening windows will introduce moisture which may force the air conditioner to work harder to remove. Do not leave a home sealed and unventilated for long periods of time, especially in humid climates, because this promotes mold growth.

4. If you use an air conditioner, leave storm windows and storm doors in place. They keep cool air inside when it's hot out, just as they keep warm air inside during winter. However, you may want to remove some of the storm windows so you can open the windows for ventilation on days when air conditioning isn't needed—even if you rely primarily on air conditioning.

5. If you experience condensation (moisture build-up) on interior surfaces, raise your air conditioning set point temperature and have a professional check your ducts for leakage and balanced airflow to all rooms.

During the heating season:

1. Open the drapes or shades on the sunny side of the house during the daytime to gather as much solar heat as possible—then close those drapes or shades at night to reduce heat loss.

2. Set back the thermostat at night and when the home is unoccupied. Every degree the heat is lowered saves you up to 5% on heating costs. (Heat pumps should only be set back 5° to prevent excessive use of backup electric heating.) Save energy by installing a programmable thermostat that can automatically adjust the temperature based on your pre-selected settings.

   When purchasing a programmable thermostat, look for ENERGY STAR qualified models, which carry the ENERGY STAR logo on the product or the box. These models are among the most energy-efficient units sold.

3. To prevent heated air from going up the chimney, keep the fireplace damper closed except when you're using the fireplace. If the fireplace doesn't have a damper, the fireplace opening can be sealed with a snug-fitting cover.

4. If you see significant condensation on windows, try to increase the ventilation in your home.

All year long:

1. When the air conditioning or heat is on, keep windows and doors closed.

2. Wash only full loads of laundry in the coolest water practical, and rinse in cold water.

3. Clean the clothes dryer lint filter after every load to maximize drying efficiency. Dry full loads of clothes, but don't overload the machine.

4. Run the dishwasher with full loads, and select the air-dry dishwasher cycle.

5. Reduce hot water waste. Don't leave the water running while brushing your teeth or shaving.

6. Turn the water heater off when everyone will be gone longer than a week.

7. Turn off lights, televisions, and stereos when you leave the room. Plug televisions and stereos into a power strip that can be switched off to eliminate stand-by power consumption. It will take equipment slightly longer to turn on, but will save the energy this equipment uses even when it is turned off.

8. Turn bath and kitchen exhaust fans on to exhaust moisture during bathing and cooking.

9. Turn off outdoor lighting during the day. (See page 18 for more on photo-sensor controls.)

10. Use natural daylight indoors during the daytime by opening the drapes or shades.

11. Maintain your refrigerator at an optimal temperature setting: 37° to 40° for the refrigerator compartment and 0° to 5° for the freezer.

12. Cover liquids and wrap foods stored in the refrigerator. Uncovered foods release moisture and make the refrigerator work harder.

13. Reduce or eliminate the use of high-energy-use appliances, such as a second refrigerator.

FOR MORE INFORMATION

Publications

- *Your Mobile Home: Energy and Repair Guide for Manufactured Housing*, by John Krigger, Saturn Resource Management, Helena, MT (www.residential-energy.com). This comprehensive and detailed guidebook contains many photographs and diagrams to explain repair and upgrade procedures. It is geared towards the handy do-it-yourselfer, but is very useful for any owner of a manufactured home. Specific items of interest include cleaning a water heater tank, making wood-framed storm windows, repairing primary windows, and insulating.

- *Consumer Guide to Home Energy Savings, 8th Edition*, by Alex Wilson, Jennifer Thorne, and John Morrill, American Council for an Energy Efficient Economy, 2003 (www.aceee.org). This 247-page guide is written in plain English and is full of tips on energy-saving strategies. Of particular interest is the detailed information on when and how to select a new furnace, air conditioner and water heater.

- *DOE Energy Savers Booklets* (www.eere.energy.gov/energy_savers). This free booklet provides easy, practical solutions for saving energy throughout the home—from insulation to appliances and lighting. It is available in English and Spanish and can be downloaded from the Web site or ordered by calling 1-877-EERE-INF (1-877-337-3463).

- *Weatherization Field Guide for Pennsylvania*, Pennsylvania Weatherization Assistance Center, 2004 (www.pct.edu/wtc). This handbook is used to train weatherization contractors working in Pennsylvania. It contains a special chapter on manufactured homes and contains a great deal of detail on insulating manufactured homes. Free from the Web site.

Web sites

- Weatherization Assistance Program (www.eere.energy.gov/weatherization). This web site provides information about the Weatherization Assistance Program, which offers energy-saving assistance to low-income families.

- Weatherization Assistance Program Technical Assistance Center (www.waptac.org). This web site links to the manufactured home energy audit tool (WX Assistant), which provides savings-to-investment ratios for many energy efficiency upgrades customized for your home as well as a refrigerator replacement analysis tool.

- HUD Energy Efficient Rehab Advisor (www.rehabadvisor.pathnet.org/index.asp). This Web site recommends energy efficiency measures for many types of rehab projects. It estimates costs, energy savings and additional benefits. Users should keep in mind that it is based on site–built construction, not manufactured homes.

- EERE Energy Savers (www.eere.energy.gov/consumerinfo). This U.S. Department of Energy Web site is a gateway to consumer information on energy efficiency and renewable energy.

- Home Energy Saver (hes.lbl.gov). This web site provides a do-it-yourself, Web-based home energy auditing tool.

- ENERGY STAR (www.energystar.gov). This web site will help you research a wide variety of ENERGY STAR qualified products and also find remodeling contractors.

- Partnerships for Home Energy Efficiency (www.energysavers.gov). Partnerships for Home Energy Efficiency is a joint effort of the U.S. Department of Energy, the U.S. Environmental Protection Agency, and the U.S. Department of Housing and Urban Development focusing on energy saving solutions for homeowners, contractors & builders, building managers, realtors, and state agencies.

- California Consumer Energy Center Consumer Energy Tips (www.consumerenergycenter.org). This web site contains numerous energy-savings tips and recommendations.

- *Home Energy Magazine*, Berkeley, CA (www.homeenergy.org). The Web site for this magazine contains many back issues in a searchable database. These articles provide practical advice on specific topics.

- Nordyne (www.nordyne.com). Contact Nordyne for copies of operating and service manuals for Intertherm and Miller heating and cooling equipment. The Web site also contains tips for selecting a heating and air conditioning contractor and recommendations for what should be included in an annual maintenance agreement.

- York International (www.york.com). Contact York for copies of operating and service manuals for York heating and cooling equipment.

- Coleman (www.colemanac.com). Contact Coleman for copies of operating and service manuals for Coleman heating and cooling equipment.

www.ingramcontent.com/pod-product-compliance
Lightning Source LLC
Chambersburg PA
CBHW081538280526
45788CB00010B/3285